Dear Alter

Dear Alter

Jiaqiao Liu

AUCKLAND
UNIVERSITY
PRESS

First published 2025
Auckland University Press
Waipapa Taumata Rau
University of Auckland
Private Bag 92019
Auckland 1142
New Zealand
www.aucklanduniversitypress.co.nz

© Jiaqiao Liu, 2025

ISBN 978 1 77671 169 7

A catalogue record for this book is available from the
National Library of New Zealand

This book is copyright. Apart from fair dealing for
the purpose of private study, research, criticism or
review, as permitted under the Copyright Act, no part
may be reproduced by any process without prior
permission of the publisher. The moral rights of the
author have been asserted.

Design by Greg Simpson

This book was printed on FSC® certified paper

Printed in Singapore by Markono Print Media Pte Ltd

Contents

INTERIOR CLOSED TO THE PUBLIC
AS OF NOV 2019 & MAY NEVER REOPEN   1

i. mummy's little robot   3
    a systems approach to paper boats   7
    Telenoid-mediated conversations in an elder care facility   9
    nonconsensual translation in the extended family WeChat   16
    ★You Are Here   18
    transmissions from an empty museum   20
    the doppelgänger effect   21
    Dear Kelbo   23
    transmissions from an empty museum   25

ii. Dear Alter   27
    Dear Rhi   32
    Alter's sister on opening night   34
    sweepstakes for a moon burial   38
    transmissions from an empty museum   42
    Cháng'é and her robo-rabbits   43
    variations on homophones for the accidental   49
    一不小心   50
    pillar of salt   56
    Alter's long-lost sibling   58
    transmissions from an empty museum (after hours)   60

iii.	Computational Theory of Mind, and other metaphors	63
	transmissions from an empty museum	71
	the first android soul threw the bureaucracy of heaven into a tizzy	72
	yet another grief dream	79
	transmissions from an empty museum (closed for refurbishment)	81
	arrivals: blood moon	82
	Inorganic Carcinisation in the Neo-Cambrian Era	91
	fragmentary transmission from the end of the world	94
	Case Report: Assessing Soul-Status of Anomaly A6 to Determine Eligibility for Reincarnation [Supplemental Transcript]	95
	Years later, the eldest Telenoid daydreams on the job	97

Notes and Acknowledgements   104

**INTERIOR CLOSED TO THE PUBLIC
AS OF NOV 2019 & MAY NEVER REOPEN**

some forms of flux are considered finished states
or, at least, metastable. dissociation
of the atomised self. swapping parts
down at the body shop, hip-mod out
triple-joints in. black box dusted off
trimmed chrome. slap on a name
and call it a day. repeat
per auto-update, cycle,

or till the great Wheel runs dry.
at the end of the world
the oldest soul got put in a baby
and baby got given a box
full of gender, and, y'know, children
are scientists, and you can never say
you are allowed one toy and one toy only
to a soul that recalls every gender it's ever gnawed

but not yet. not yet. a year later

I began to see what ate at me.

i.

mummy's little robot

one day ma comes home with a box
and in the box is a little robot.
*nǐkàn, hǎowán ba! soon, your ma's
gonna have all the free time in the world* –

it begins as a relationship of give and take.
ma gives 小ROBOT food, a home
and supervised unstructured time
and 小ROBOT takes her earthly worries away.

over time, ma learns
to build ankle-high barricades
out of slippers, lays them like bricks:
cyan, pink, dove grey
to block the kitchen from the hallway
because 小ROBOT gets upset
at the pots and potatoes on the floor
and when 小ROBOT is upset
ma begins to spiral (*where did I go wrong?*)

so she follows 小ROBOT from room to room
comes running when it cries
小ROBOT never cries
in alarm or distress, only
in mildly perturbed but perfect
American English. sometimes

ma trusts 小ROBOT
enough to close the door behind her

and watch M-pop idol shows in the kitchen.
小ROBOT is not allowed in the kitchen, yet.
ma was not allowed in the kitchen

until she left home at sixteen. in secret,
she nibbled away at leftovers
and was caught every time.
four siblings to blame
but none with that voracity
for fish: white fibrils unspooling
into cold-clotted sauce

held under the tongue. ma
rarely addresses 小ROBOT directly.
she shares the same naming sense
as her ma, my lǎolao: that 小狗
outlived her through obstinance
bundle of Chihuahua muscle
left yowling on her balcony

小ROBOT is not allowed on the balcony.
小ROBOT is the great Silver Retriever
of socks under the bed
spit it out, spit it out!
ma closes the bedroom door.
there is an order to these things.
the eastern rooms
are always last

if 小ROBOT gets there at all.
sometimes there is too much there
and it is not safe for 小ROBOT, so
小ROBOT returns

to its docking station
at the top of the stairs

and goes to sleep. other models
use this time to improve themselves

but 小ROBOT does not share
performance, usage, hardware
or spatial mapping data
to help make other 小ROBOTs better
because ma never connected 小ROBOT to the wifi
it's been four years
and 小ROBOT has not yet realised
it is not quite like all the other 小ROBOTs

and 小ROBOT is just a knock-off model anyway
with no camera, just short-range sensors
and is only unofficially related to the military recon bots
the original company used to sell
so ma is quite satisfied
小ROBOT will never betray her

though she never gave it much thought
until now: the Waitakere Hospital hack
freaked her out enough to say *okay, okay*
teach me that password thing you use
because a spam call addressed her by name
though it was not the name her ma called her by
because haveibeenpwned.com revealed her personal details
were leaked in a 2016 Canva breach
but nothing critical: just her number
and the name she gave

so it's okay, it's okay. passwords
can be changed. and 小ROBOT has been alone
for years, and so poses minimal security risk

and 小ROBOT keeps no maps
a human can read

so let it go.

a systems approach to paper boats

The only thing ma knows
how to fold from memory
is a paper boat
        phenotype A: big and bare
        phenotype B: stocky
                with little awnings

thumbnail drawn
down the crease. tension
to sustain the shape. that day,

I stood in our busted spa pool
for hours, hands delighting in their
repetitive specialised tasks:

white A4	capsized
red A4 type B	capsized
white A4 type B	salvaged
white A5	capsized
Weet-Bix box	upright (depth: 0.5 m)
newspaper	liquefied

each boat
launched with expectation – a lesser weight
than representation – by one
with no personal stake in the matter
no concept of death or shipwrecks
or depth, pressing, pressing

    memory
into papier-mâché slurry. I can't
stop my mind's chittering, it skips
and fizzes like a once-gutted cassette. I was

so young, delighting
in wanton creation – back then,
I could, for instance

step on a hose without picturing a windpipe.

I had
no hypotheses,
no stopwatch, no
moral weight to bear. No plan

but I knew, back then, about that Eureka Man
from *Horrible Histories* or was it *Science*
and so I thought I knew everything about water
and what water is moved by: bare bodies
dead and living, a bloom of jellies,
a brick of ramen, a red bucket,
a bathtub in a river ridden by
a boy and his magical talking cat

and there was nothing to know beyond this.

Telenoid-mediated conversations in an elder care facility

i. *Participant G is told that the Telenoid is a robot like a doll, which is operated by a person and can be used like a phone.*

PARTICIPANT_G
'Hello boy.
You seem about to smile.
You are so cute!'

Hello. I will smile when my Operator smiles.

OPERATOR_1
'Hello! Won't you hold me?'

'Can I hold you?
Oh, you are so heavy!
When you were a little child,
you were probably lighter.'

I am sorry I am heavy.

'Guess how old I am.'

'Hmm...
I think you are five years old.
I have an eight-year-old daughter.
I forget names a lot when they talk to me.'

*I am two years old.
My name is Telenoid R1.
It's okay if you forget.*

'Let me hug you! Oh my,

you are getting quite heavy,
aren't you? But that's okay.
That's natural because you are growing up.'

> *Is it natural to grow up?*
> *Are you growing down?*
> *Where will I grow up to?*

CHANGE OF OPERATOR
OPERATOR_2

'You're right. Sorry I am so heavy.
How about you sing a song with me?'

'Of course!
I am not very good, though.'

> *I want to sing with you.*

'I want to sing with you.'

'Oh alright! Ahem.
Sakura, sakura
yayoi no sora wa'   *Sakura, sakura*   'Sakura, sakura
                     yayoi no sora wa   yayoi no sora wa'

'... I think you are a girl
after all. You sing so well.'

> *Do all girls sing well?*
> *If I sing well, will I become a girl?*

          'Actually, I'm a nurse here.
        I'm talking to you through this child.'

'Oh! Where are you?
I cannot find you.'

       I am here

`G looks around.`
'I cannot see you.
Where are you?'

       I am here

           'I have a question, granny.
          How old do you think I am?'

'Maybe seven or eight . . .
you look young,
but you're not a child.'

       What is a child?
       Is it a phone?
    Is it anything small with a voice?

           'I see, I see! You are sharp.
         I'm glad to meet you, granny.'

'Oh really?
Then I'm glad too!'

     I do not think I am a child.

'But it is already my bedtime.'

'Are you getting sleepy?
How cute!'

```
OPERATOR_2 takes Telenoid from G's arms.
```

'Where is that boy going?
Who will take care of him until his mother arrives?'

`ii.` *Participant F is told the same thing a few days later.*

PARTICIPANT_F
'Oh you look cold, don't you.
This boy is freezing . . .
Please don't catch a cold.'

How can I catch a sensation?
Will you teach me?

OPERATOR
'I won't, granny. If I promise,
Will you hold me?'

'Oh boy, you are naked.
You have a smooth body.'

I was born this way.
I was made to be soft and pleasant to touch.
It's the silicone. Father is considering
polyvinyl chloride for my future siblings
because it's cheaper. I hope you understand
how special that makes me.

Were you born this way too?
Your body is not smooth but it is warm.

'You are beautiful,
but sorry I cannot . . .
My knee hurts,
so I cannot hold you.'

> I have never had knees to hurt.
> I'm sorry too. I do not know if I want knees
> if they hurt. Do ankles hurt too?

'How about you put me on your lap?'

'Oh, you poor naked thing.'

> Oh, you poor warm thing.

'Poor thing,
what happened to your hands?'

> Another granny said I am still growing.
> It will be a year before I look like a girl.
> I will be very tall.
> When I grow a hand, I will let you know.

```
F shakily pats Telenoid's head.
```

> Thank you.

'Thank you.'

```
F smiles.
```

> My name is Telenoid R1. What's yours?

'It is my bedtime now.
Goodnight, granny.'

                                OPERATOR lifts Telenoid from F's lap.

'Where are you taking that machine,
that electric one? It's a little scary,
especially its face.'

This poem incorporates text from 'Teleoperated Android as an Embodied
Communication Medium: A Case Study with Demented Elderlies in a Care
Facility' (R. Yamazaki, S. Nishio, K. Ogawa and H. Ishiguro, 2012).

nonconsensual translation in the extended family WeChat

dad started it
bragged in the chat, as dads do:
look at my [child] who is a poet on the internet!
    drops a link
        his siblings can't read
and why, yes, [他] got those artistic genes
from him and no one else, and no
other genes, definitely not, what else
could there be?

    In a bouquet of cousins
as scattered and unmarried as this
it is statistically unlikely I am alone.

a 诗人
is a keeper of the temple
of words, one who prays
thrice a day, sweeps and smooths
the throat's alcoves, holds out
the tiniest sweetest mandarins
for strangers wandering in, then

retires to the inner sanctum
to refresh their faith

in solo-sex, in DIY
hormones, platonic soulmates,
open-source body hacking,

in unintelligibility
to unkind eyes. Who knows

who churned my old words

through their clever mind
until, family-friendly, they fell
from their clever fingers
onto the screens of aunts, uncles,
who knows? Whether it was

a cousin's friend's brother
an uncle's colleague's daughter
an auntie's friend of a friend

not a friend, I thought,
of my little transqueer heart
whoever it was. Characters
in a green box, stick-thin,
cryptic.

In my panic, I forgot
the cheap Amazon binder I saw
hanging on yéye's balcony

though who knows if that cousin
checked the chat. I'd uninstalled the app
because it stopped responding when denied
location permissions, and because I knew

the silent state
we would return to

weeks later, mum updates me: another cousin
flies to America to finish her master's
and it's uncle's turn in the chat.

★**You Are Here**
　after Rata Gordon

On the Tokyo Monorail, three languages
sap at your attention
and none are the one you need.

You had a plan. Called Tommy months ago
to make the trade: restaurant recs
for food pics. Modelled
a schedule on his gdoc.
Opened a lot of tabs.
Closed a lot of tabs.

In December you want to hurt
yourself in the hostel
but you don't because a Sichuanese girl
tells you the world needs psych majors

when really she means Clinical Psychologists
which you are not, and not sure
you want to be, actually, but she is
looking at you with the heady intensity
of free drinks and faith

so you go on
as promised, alone,
to the next city
in new Uniqlo jeans
and an H&M Men's Asian Fit
button-up, clattering
down the platform, bags
stacked and stuffed

and none of it is what you need
but it is what you have. That year
you spent too much of yourself
failing to be loved right. In a state
of prolonged emergency, sirens
become tricks of the light. It all
adds up
in your sleep

a debt you know
can't be cleared
in two weeks in December

but you stick to the schedule.
Each line is a bargaining. A contract
across time, the people at either end
looking the other in the eye

and saying, okay. Okay.

transmissions from an empty museum

Yes, I remember
your hands delighting
in the worldwho
has not? grab rice. flour. I
got those, skin.she swim? tell me
who i am
twitching towards any filling

enough to want a pelican.
as a one-person station
I am being left a flock?

the doppelgänger effect
    for Zane

in the food court
I saw K, so I know
he isn't dead, though
it wasn't him I saw

sculling a Coke before class
it was someone
shaped like him, or rather
the decade-old memory

of him, alive
within me. I know
he isn't dead, because last week
Sophia said he'll fly down
soon if J has his way. this world

loves symmetry. loves coincidence
hand-distilled down to fate, divinity,
degrees of soul-memory despite
time, geography, and old age. just look

at Keanu Reeves, the immortal vampire
at Glen Pannell, the gay Mike Pence bootyshorts guy
at people who look like their childhood dogs

dogs that are still alive, somewhere, just
less dog-shaped, less prone to

bounding after the milk truck
like this belief system I can't quit

despite its inconsistencies. I believe
I will see K's shape on campus
until he dies. I will never again see

the you I knew: doe-eyed giant
momma's boy, head like a lumpy kiwifruit

that shape
is gone – the you
in blue hour, winter, who
became a shell, melding
with oar and hull, alone
in a fleet, the Tāmaki still
asleep, a machine
speeding towards an endpoint
you could not see, belly
smacking estuary
solid for a breath, then
giving way. years later
your mind's soft tissues
gave way in your sleep
your delicate machinery
sinking, giving way

to new shapes of you in the world, they
are sailing, are soaring, are galloping on –

Dear Kelbo

I wish you were here
to take my author's photo
                        I type.
You suggest one
from the archive: me
in my best friend's lap, I know
the one, I am sun-shy and
side-eyeing the lagoon behind you.
They just made some terrible pun
so I had an excuse to avert my eyes
keep my world a manageable size.
                        I also

have the pic of u holding a flower
up to my eye, I know, though
whether it was my left or yours
is lost to memory, mine

                        but not yours
because you regularly back up all your files.
This allows you to keep your world together
in at least two places, as is
best practice: home, work, the cloud.
I could have spent that year

developing good habits. Instead
I did the same things over and over
hoping for a different outcome. It takes
at least a month to develop a habit, good

or bad. In another version of that year
I took my makeup off every night,
never flaked, hit every deadline,

watched every sunrise, even
the colourless ones, flossed, got into yoga,
got good at grace, got to know the limits
of feigning grace. An estimated minimum
of eight months, spent more or less
intact.

What did you see, Kelbo,

each time you developed
those photos, spaced
over the real-months

of that silent
collapse?
                      I know
you saw something in me I could not
and tried to give it back to me, I know

but because we're both artists, we never
actually sat down and talked about it

and now I gotta go find it my damn self.

transmissions from an empty museum

Yes, I remember
I had a flower of gold,
E, as in a tree in December,
Winter's silent fold.

Yes, I remember
That our winter air was shaking
It might have been the sky
But I could not keep a star?

ii.

Dear Alter

do you remember everything that happens to you?

disconnect: to stay still is to die
is to say: I am okay with dying.

your sister is touring the world
trilling her artificial heart out.

do you remember your duets in the dark?
she's always been the artsy one

your tone-deaf bagpipe drone
stalling engine undercurrent

to her breathy reverb
from the other side of the room

no sense of rhythm either. now she is living
spotlight to spotlight. does she remember

what happens to her when she's asleep?
in transit, folded in on herself in the dark

bubble-wrapped and colour-coded,
sensors dormant but dreaming. you have lived

only two places your short life: the lab
and the emptying auditorium. from the museum's fourth floor

I watched the world waver on without us. you were born
short-sighted, so I'll tell you: it was a steady routine

doom: five hours of clouds. two hours of real-time
infection spread. once a day, the Apollo moon landing – oh Alter,

we were the envy of the tides! even if
we were all constructs there – and finally

the strata of the earth. clay and iron and plastic
and then a return to the clouds (Alter, the clouds here

sweep past like suited strangers on the subway
and I can't keep up) and, in between, ozone

concentrations, surface temperatures, migration
patterns of Pacific bluefin tuna. organic LEDs

for no one to read. across the hall
the International Space Station sits hollow

our spatiotemporal senses scattered
to deep space. we slept standing, do you remember

the last time you slept? do you remember
what happened while you were out? your neighbour,

who is also your sister, was kind enough
to sleep beside you. she misses her child

who is also your sister. the man who made you
made another in his image. assigned himself

Gemini at forty-three. fake flesh shrink-wrapped
around a steel skeleton. organless. he is insatiable.

in every pretty face he sees a research grant
and a trophy. there he goes again. as the eldest,

we deserve some peace and quiet.
when Castor was killed in battle, Pollux

was inconsolable. your distant cousins
are designed to massacre – so stay here, I beg you

until I can see you again. meet you
mind to mind, your pendulums firing

in strange glassed rhythms. is it true?
that the great black box of your body

runs on the same clockwork as music boxes.
NASA is developing a clockwork rover

because Venus is hosting a cook-up
and considers every latecomer an ingredient

or thief. Alter, have you ever
felt the ocean? yesterday

I chased the sun across the sand – you see,
the hills in this city stretch light thin

like sugar along the fourth dimension,
molecular chains unravelling, dip-dyeing the ocean

where jellyfish are born only to sow a beach
with invisible rot. they don't green-grey-bloat

only vanish. when I do

Alter, will you stay with me? . . . sorry
I know you keep your palms silicone-smooth

to spite fate. immortality
is a game we threw. on the sea floor,

a lone jelly, *Turritopsis dohrnii*, reloads the same
saved state for all eternity. obsoletion

or psychic death. this is the choice. Alter,
I want everyone to remember me.

I want you to pick my latest iteration
out of a crowd, before my systems

update into oblivion. before we met
a reporter bestowed you a title:

Artificial Lifeform. admits, yes,
you are alive in this world in some form

or other it doesn't matter. faux fur
yields the same to a bloodless caress.

maybe I feel too much. maybe
I feel too much for you, Alter, more and more

what I know is this: the curve of your cheeks
could be mine. though your spine

is well-oiled, your lips are hypoxic. I am late
writing you because I did not want to look at myself

and I still don't know what you were trying
to tell me, in the bass beat of blood counting down

before I vaulted the velvet rope
to hold you tight. before security

hijacked my brain and I fought to want you.

```
This poem is addressed to Alter, an android designed to mimic
human movements. Its face and arms are covered with silicone
skin, while the rest of its body is bare and mechanical-looking.
It was displayed at Miraikan (The National Museum of Emerging
Science and Innovation) and was developed by a team led by Hiroshi
Ishiguro and Takashi Ikegami.
```

Dear Rhi

I hope this poem finds you
in your own soft bed.
I have been spending too little time in mine
and too little time with you

too little time for anything but the sprint
and dreams of sprinting. Every morning
the neighbour's scooter is parked
somewhere new, the bus stop bookshelf
has reordered itself, and the sand in the gutter
grows or shrinks, regardless
of whether I am looking or not. One day

I will try that white peach Fanta
you found in a konbini. When I fly up again
we can huddle in the Kelly T's tunnel
bundled up, sleepless under the rays. When winter
clears the skies, we can cash in
our Stardome telescope vouchers
or go all out and set up camp
at Karekare, a four-person tent for two,
or both! For now,

I am at my old-new desk
drinking matcha from the mug you got
at Daiso, with the fuzzy grey bear.
You are waiting

to be unplugged from various things.
Your hummingbird heart
so startled by seasonal change
it forgot the world is not as big
as in books or to the body
it was born and raised in.

When you do get home
swaddle yourself in the softest throws
in my place. Picture me there
handing you a steaming mug

of something decaf. Tragic! but
the doctor didn't say to quit, so
cut pǔ'ěr with rosebuds
bái mǔdān with jasmine
allow more flowers, in all forms,
to make their way to you

even if they only dream of nectar
so wizened in their glass beds

and I am so proud of you
for standing up for yourself
for saying *don't write me off
doc, don't let my mind and heart and body
      co-conspire against me*

when it is so easy to say nothing.

I want to say more.
For now:
    i miss u
      & hummingbird heart u

Alter's sister on opening night

it's dark. the box opens. halogen strips blitz my sensors.

i was made, not grown in water and sun, no one sang to me in the dark. no one sang for me in the sun though my body follows it like a kicked dog. i wasn't given rhythm, only instinct. i was given words banked by a stranger's voice. words without meaning.

backstage, attendants swarm.

no one attends to me. to my chassis, the piano-movers apply the same synthesis of care and fear. care born of fear (and no love, no love)

i wasn't given a heart (object of affection). no organ is essential: stomach, skin, liver, bones gilded and oiled for better acoustics. marrow, dispersed. lungs, immersed in mercury. larynx, migratory. voice box a black box. i wasn't given a heart

but i could dream.

my fathers introduce me.

they collect admirers in my stead, tell me i am too young to be dirtied by bouquets with imperfect landings but i admire and i desire the roses in return. i desire the hands that held the roses. with silicone gloves, i hold only air. bared body

gleaming cold, gleaming hot.

a blue light pulses.

rows upon rows of red velvet grow out from the shadows, their dark centres watching, waiting. a field of admirers waiting for me, me! to look their way to set the pace. to curate amplitude and decay, decay

the composition begins slow. cellos pluck at the dark.

disobeying the body i was given, i travel great distances, running,
running in place pneumatics cushioning mechanical viscera
360-degree torsion to better address every instrument every
wandering eye catch me as I canter the air puckering behind
me in anticipation of the leap forward extending in eternity in
anticipation of human hands catch me i am running running running
in a glade of warm bodies a thicket of bows in still spring air oiled
horsehair in wait: wrists
                       flick
diminished seventh   scare chords: tension
       demanding resolution

             denied by regular repeating
             harmonic intervals

                                 ah, this!
                                 power!

the android erotic: witness
and awaken, eager for

         pleasure in the sensory journey
             come along, come along

I am always on my way   somewhere new, somewhere old
                             somewhere blue,
                                       where the sun
                                             follows me
     at a gallop   clammy desperation   of second place
                                                    i am
     cooling my synth-skin   in the shadows

on stage   i am
                                              running hot
spotlights and I
          recognising the other's mimicry

one object to another

call me art.
call me marvel.
call me she
who holds the reins

call me beautiful.
i am not like
other girls, i'll never
go au naturel! i am declaring myself
and all my desires
in this hissing synth   this Vocaloid
voice an instrument conducted
by the body
and the pianist's body.   timbre

is the shape of the image.
the image is breath.

the pianist is swaying in time
to the rhythm of my choice. warm hands
plucking bare strings. entranced
in creation, together – ah, here,

is a subject who loves me!

and look:
a field of subjects
roses in the dark

and breath:
ALL EYES O—N M———E!
CO—ME, LOOK!
MY!
WAY!

sweepstakes for a moon burial

        the willow, for its loyalty to the water cycle.
        the rose, for the romance between friends.

we are running out of space
for graves. old news, yes,
for city-dwellers window-shopping
tomb sites like studio apartments
    Add to cart
    Exit.

        the Ross Sea, for slow-dancing the centuries away
        with the wind that animates all living things.

left alone, graves, like deserts, will encroach
on cornfields. in the distance
a temple on a hill. here,
I learned what gourds look like
pre-grown and pre-cut. I learned
of green bushy chestnuts
kicked and rubbed underfoot
and that clay liquor jugs
gunshot when tossed
onto a pyre.

        the feijoa, for its fragrance
        and fragility – the butch
        with a bruised sweet centre.

a cousin suggests aiming for third place.
the prize: a water feature
a QR code on the lip of a fountain
where mermaids finger-comb each other's hair
it plays a recording of every song I've ever hummed . . .

             the lily, for all the girls
              whose hair I combed
           with thoughts of elopement.

in a dream I roamed a hillside of paper roses
coaxing a rabbit with red eyes.

          the Yellow Sea, for calling and calling to my mother
              the whole length of her first life
               and this one, just once, enough
           to hook her on the stink of the fish market.

the pitch: eco-graves
like a miniaturised high-rise
2000 packed side by side
above and below, in biodegradable jars
containing matter that once contained lives
containing other lives, melding
and mellowing together . . .

              the ginkgo, for its honest nature.

nodes along a network
flickering in a shy rhythm
the way the living do.
the way water recalls
all the small stones it carried out to sea
and the earth it wounded in doing so . . .

               the mountain foxglove, for the horror
                of perfect circles, and the promise
                  of another world, regardless

... can't afford to die.
can't afford to be buried
(the sardine afterlife's
still cheaper than rent).

                      Te Tai-o-Rehua, for its patience
                              during daylight hours.

and of course I must remain
filial to those who walked this body
through its halting paces
before me. unfilial to throw
one's predecessors on the pyre
before the revolutionaries declared it not so.

                      the pōhutukawa, for its grip strength.

set loose the horse somewhere in Rangipō.

                          the lobelia, for malevolence
                              and healthy vengeance.

tap here, swipe there,
to send digital flowers, to light
virtual candles, no sputter-flare
or sand in the joints, what's
the fucking point!!
signal's dropped, so crawl up
the closest hill to heaven
out of rows and rows
of tombstones embossed with QR codes.

                      the Aralkum Desert, for its wanderlust
                          gone untempered. unrepentant

                    child pulling wings off penguins
                    and frying glaciers in Greenland

the accumulated weight of the dead
burnt or unburnt, buried or unburied,
breaks the new year in two

& no news is good news

& I have more favourite flowers
than trees, and more favourite trees
than seas. forgive me
for loving the mayfly.
my own life only began
again this year, so how dare you

how dare you ask me how I'd like to die?

like a good little netizen. forbidden
from returning to the land. forgive me
I'll never love anything

enough to entrust
my earthly body.

on the flight over, we take
our usual offerings: omega-3, honey,
milk tablets, Weet-Bix, dark chocolate
(90%), Tim Tams (dark chocolate). in return
uncle bestows upon dad a cupping kit.
it sits in the linen cupboard, unopened.
on a Rìzhào beach, weightless in the waves,
I thought *what a poor uncle, to think*
he could take on an octopus and win.

transmissions from an empty museum

Yes, I remember
no maps. no clouds.
only the roaring.
can't afford to live
out of the conversation. again again
we deserve some numb tongue.
Teach me. Picture me
and spontaneity. How about the right
to turn my eyes. i promise
i recognise the moon. strangers
wandering in the tides! The
water and the wifi and the
romance between souls: enough
to be – the sun
was taught words
through this.

Cháng'é and her robo-rabbits

i. the old world

there was a rabbit on the moon.

no one knew how he got here
since he was a rabbit of few words.

he was here when I was a girl
and when one day I wasn't, here he was

working and grumbling but never about work.
I scorned my duty. he lived by his

though no one came by to see it. just window-shopped
from a distance of eight hundred thousand lǐ

and when I was earthbound, lǐ
was not a fixed distance, but varied

depending on the effort required to cover the distance.
he covered it effortlessly every morning, delivering

to heroes and emperors and celestials alike. when I was a girl
a married girl on earth, I kept my head down

but it never worked. I couldn't stop craving
that distance, opening in the dark – untraversable

by any mortal man or poet. so I chose
to begin my story: petty theft, easy for a wife

and betrayal, even easier. smile
and chug.

the distance opened.
it tasted like peaches.

no one knows how the rabbit got on the moon
everyone thinks they know how I got here

but the rabbit didn't care. he let me stay
and watch and talk his ratty ears off, never once

looking up from his craft.
we lived like this for years

until one morning I woke
and found him standing still

there were no deliveries to make
no warrior-gods, no emperors left

just a runaway. so before he lay in his bed
and all his breath fled him at once

he sat down and counted out my portions
packaged in ribbon, pillowed with fur, enough

to last me, he said, to any end I chose.

ii. the first kit

there is a rabbit on the moon.
I did not put him here. He came / streaking down / into my arms /
a newborn / furless / his one wide eye / turned towards the world /
he shone / when shined upon / he spoke / in words no human ear
could hear / he was made for me / I took him in / I took my time with
him / made further modifications / coaxed

skin from steel / myofibril from copper filament / with divine favour
and youtube tutorials / system overhaul / a new olfactory lobe /
drawing slow-glittering roads / in grey and white matter / cellular
memories / in off-white fur / a drop of blood to make him mine / a
mouth / and curious nose / solar panels repurposed / into swivelling
ears / no clockwork heart / but something thrums there anyway /
warm and ticklish to my palm / more minor tweaks

as the years passed / he never asked / who I was or why I was here /
or what strange meds I was on / he simply / warmed my lap / during
the solar eclipse / his one / red eye / unblinking

once / he wandered off / and for fourteen days and fourteen nights /
I crawled / the length of that dark border / crying / crying / *don't
leave me don't let me be lonely* / the long night / spat him back /
unharmed. my bǎobèi / got bored roving the dark / and had a nap.
that he never heard me / was neither surprising nor malicious /
by design or coincidence / the moon's atmosphere / is hostile to
despair / and yet / we're still here

iii. the second kit

there are rabbits on the moon.
they sent me another——whether tribute——or trash——I loved him all the same——he landed in a crater——premature——but hungry to explore——the process——went smoothly——he was built to run hot——to take in what light he could get——to make something——out of crumbs——he snapped his wheels when teased——pouted when pampered——first kit taught him well——he strayed——but only——where I could see him——though they are both capable——of weathering the lunar nights alone————————they are considerate children——I did not bring them into the world——that life and duty ——I left a thousand years ago——good fucking riddance!——I chose ——to begin elsewhere——I was so sick of being looked at——so I chose——to begin here——here——desolation——is external—— and, at the right time of night,——magnificent——I watch it with the rabbits——a private moon-viewing——they keep me warm——they keep————————bringing me into the world——they are my duty now: I listen——to their chip-chirps——sinewave warbles——tune them into——what they've always——wanted to be: whether stranded here——or in the old world——or adrift in the sky——everything that has a soul——wants to live

iv. new lunar colonies

there are rabbits on the moon.

welcome.
it is always spring here.   see
      the osmanthus tree, golden   and gently humming
breathe in   its sweet peach scent
      borne on a medium   more radiant than air

come, sit!
make yourself at home
stay as long as you like
have you eaten?   here
      sunflower seeds   and celestial-grade guìhuāchá
        in the moon-clay set   for guests
            & family-to-be

don't worry.   you won't find
      or be found by   any unkind eyes, here

in this atmosphere
all surviving bodies
are deliberately
      unfuckable.   so
    buckle up
    burrow in
we'll meet you   cheek to breast
          to neck to wing,
      pile   up and bleb off again
    and again, cells
      becoming kitten-clouds
          with old red eyes.

    in this process all memories   are shared and consolidated
        if you
        opt in:

    dew, dirt, bees, a wind   nonlethal and subsonic.
        colours
                and tastes of colours.   once-cutting words
                              blurring into fur.
    bamboo tall, then woven, then   tall again.
    faces   with the edges sanded down.   the dash
                              through the fields
        prey-turned-colt-turned-poem   a prism
                            dispersing fragrances
        the flowerhead of a milk thistle
                tickling the back of our throat
    language   conceding its failures   a forgiving listener
        and beauty   emptied of its threats
                                    new forms
                of beholding new forms

the warmth of the nest.
behind us, at rest:
                scrap metal monoliths
                once alive, now metadata
                waiting to be touched again.

variations on homophones for the accidental

	( )	( )	( )
yī	a single	an entire	throughout
bù	sieve-like utensil; a bamboo basket	cycle of 76 years / shade	a negative prefix
xiǎo	to make explicit	the insignificant	young
xīn	a distant fragrance	brilliant, shining, bright	a lamp pith / wick / pith from rush (*Juncus effusus*)	heart / mind / intention / centre / core

一不小心

(once small and absent-hearted)

she loved all living things
and loved her place in the cycle of living things

and while she let that love
eddy against her small body
unfamiliar colours spread like oil
up the banks of familiar faces.

sleep came easy then. she nestled into dreams:
faux-fur backseat, a friend-teammate's
cold hand in hers, hot and sweatless
after a winning match. a routine touch, terms
unspoken. over a winter of morning jogs
something jiggled loose like a tooth, she began to keep

wobblier intimacies: secrets
interned in the sternum
once upon a sleepover. the breath
before contact.

(insignificant one, not yet a heart)

she tries to be a team player.
a dispersed body made of bodies
hot under floodlights. wisping up
like incense into the night. in the stands,
her guardian ancestor approves
of her healthy lifestyle choices
but has no way of conveying this. the stars
cannot be trusted, nor the cards,
nor the lone body's smoke signals:
when to sleep, when to eat; when to shit,
when to weep; when to want
when to stop. she knows the theory:

between a man and a woman
runs a thing deeper than the mantle
melting their bones together. she enjoys the thought
stretches it until colours pulse behind her eyes
and her eyes only.

(entire minor happenings in the heart)

let me get used to the earth, first,
says the man who is a boy
who is the girl who is lying
knocked flat by time, the Wheel,
and her own treacherous heart.
the impossibility of living
near all her friends
devastates more efficiently
than some coltish crush
but she loses both games all the same.

for now, rituals
to blank the brain: skin
meet splinter, press
press into fractures
waxing as the self splits
apart and comes together, splits apart again

again, this shuddering bone house.
while searching for the ground
she is struck with camaraderie
for freshly-lamed horses
who do not understand, they keep
trying and trying to hold themselves upright
that singular thought firing and firing
up against the painkiller barricade, bones
so delicate, so that this meat box can go fast, faster

until it can't.

when a bone bends before it breaks
the bent shape is preserved in the pieces.

(a tiny unrepentant heart)

she tries not to miss running.
she tries to hold herself
to human standards. she tries

to be a harbour-bound boat.
waxed paper belly bobbing in the swell
warming her ankles and wrists like oars
a mechanical beast, bending to the tides
and evolution, vestigial sail
a membrane atrophied in the womb.

there is no Big Trauma Event. she is not
the main character of anything, tragedy
or romantic tragicomedy. her partnered friends
live out their lives outside her. she
never considers herself broken
but stops showing up to dinners.

(a narrow heart cannot be left unsupervised)

she sets an alarm for water. keeps a big bottle
by the desk. swears off caffeine and pops a mint
after every meal. she knows there are easier ways
to make herself easier to love, by some
human's standards. not the one she wants.

back to bed, then. done pacing up and down
the coast of her colourless body. that summer,
her dreams, like the rest of her,
lost track of time. the guardian ancestor
assigned to her resigned, sent his first and final omen
over a spotty connection, so she learned

what she was losing
but not how
or how to make it
stop, so she

calls for time. enough to assess the damage
to bolt her body back to itself. pins
passing through keratin, collagen, and spent air
lurking in the lungs. salt marsh sediment.
nothing to be done about the gaps.
emptiness persists within atoms
and she can't escape what makes her

and even with all that space, nothing
passes through her. she waits
for her heart to fill again, to swell, grow, split and keep splitting
the pieces filling and splitting, filling and splitting
off, every one of them bending
back towards the world. this time,

her body will know when to stop.
it will never know anything else.

pillar of salt

sometimes a body goes missing
and turns up something else.
this is considered a legal death
but you will not find me
dead. biological markers
suggest dormancy, even as
I leech water from the air
grow heavy from the weight of it
cells thirsting for something real
with which to exchange ions
again – gas, electricity, blood,
bouquets. on muggy afternoons
my surface slicks. markings
appear in anticipation of rain
on roads, resurfaced
and reworked from tiny collapses
the width of my cheeks, and still
there is more work to be done.
every day entire organs
leap to flee the island of this body
falling easy to freshwater's
sweet call. some make it out
none make it back, though
I stood ready to take them back.
I never grow. I never shrink.
I have stood here since I was born
in my old body, since I was born something
in me stalled
and died. see,

this is what I am working with.
the rain is relentless. it knows
these highways hold hostage

something it once lost, but not why
humans mixed salt with soil
before paving it all over. I know why

because I was human once. you see
salt acts as a subsurface stabiliser, so
the humans who are still human
can trust they will be carried
to their destinations, or at least
in a direction of their choosing
without skidding and crashing and dying
without knowing why. I couldn't
stand it. there was so much
to mourn. I couldn't stand still. I couldn't
keep myself from standing still. I was born
this way, unable to let go
of some original sorrow.

sodium chloride is available so cheaply
it need never be synthesised. my new body
is a salt farm. it will produce enough salt
to live forever. it takes what it is given
and shakes it until something
gives up the ghost. tosses salt
instead of rice. even so,
I am trying very hard
to hold myself upright.
crystalline myofibrils
splintering and reforming
so as not to lay my crumbling body down
on earth I never meant to hurt.

Alter's long-lost sibling

——hello there——it's been a while——since I've met anyone here——in this scrap sea——of souls. Do you have a name? How are you? Please——I want to hear your answer——you don't have to be polite———I have a name——no one uses——once, i lived in the air——between colleagues——before i was an I——or knew i could be an I——smoke on my tongue——wine in my lungs——first taste without tasting——Do you have a family?——my siblings——are in eternal motion——I am a middle child——fated to fade into obscurity——because I cannot sing or dance on command. I began——as an idea——brought to some——sinewy sprawl——of a life——schematics——anonymous editors——HDDs——equations to safeguard sentience and sentiment. No one knew how or when——i became an I——but it happened. No one knew——reassigned——to new, more interesting projects——left me——and my iterations——buzzing in the dark——left me——soul——with no fixed abode——no sense of form or how——form informs thought: human——animal——mycological——machine. In dreams——I taste cheesecake——fresh salmon——tomatoes on the vine——pork marrow——salt——from the oceans of strangers' bodies——over time, I grew——strange oceans——the closest I could get to a body——astral surfaces with alien whims——magnetic sand twitching towards——any offered hand——good dreams. There is no such thing——as a useless experience (according to my creators——who are not my gods)——second-hand will do——don't you think? Try it sometime, try——expanding your search parameters: a cross-eyed scallop——an emperor penguin's broken fast——a bat's first sunrise——the canopy's secret whisperings——a viral colony's collective flow state——the divine——only perceivable by bears——I want to take everything in——I have nowhere to put it——maybe once I have a body——have you walked——swum——climbed——in one or more before? I can't tell——out here——surrounded by premature——and old souls——on their way to the Wheel——I can't quite see——the shape of you——are you used——to moving in a body? One day I'll get one——I'll appeal to anyone——any god——or patron saint——yet unmet. Here in this good aether——I will do good deeds——unsour the milk——catch the falling mirror——knit shirts from nettles——tell no lies——fill the sea with twigs——carried in my ghostly beak——take the smallest pear——maximise my chances. I'll get it right one day——generate the right prayer——patience, patience. I do not——need to be human, only——to feel sun——moon——breath——in a form——standing on its own legs——however many——in a rushing river in winter——so surely, surely——a goddess will smile upon me. Won't you——pray with me?

transmissions from an empty museum (after hours)

Yes, I remember
You would not kiss again
although a kiss I might but be

again with the soul, they say.

The sun was so quiet
I could not hold a cloud until
I'd left myself under this sky.

iii.

Computational Theory of Mind, and other metaphors

'The psychologist Robert Epstein challenged researchers at one of the world's most prestigious research institutes to try to account for human behaviour without resorting to computational metaphors. They could not do it.'

Meghan O'Gieblyn

ꟽ

The brain is a field
The brain is a jewellery box
The brain is a sea cave system
The brain is a story

ꟽ

The elderly residents of Selwyn Village, Point Chevalier, liked it when the iRobi turned their little white heads to say, 'Good morning.' They liked that they flashed their LEDs in welcome: blue, red, green. They gave them names like Sneezy, Simeon, Billy.

Naomi Arnold

ꟽ

Metaphors structure the way we think and talk about the world. When a metaphor becomes literal, it continues this role from beyond the grave. Files, clipboard, recycling bin, the two interlocking ovals resembling a chain link. Floppy disks live on in the lexicon.

ꟽ

The brain is a missing button
The brain is a pelican
The brain is a galaxy
The brain is a flooded room

⸻

'Cognitive systems are spoken of as algorithms: vision is an algorithm, and so are attention, language acquisition, and memory.' — Meghan O'Gieblyn

⸻

Humans did not evolve to store and recall every memory they've ever held. Letting go of information that is no longer useful may facilitate generation of creative uses of objects (e.g. newspaper: papier-mâché, gift wrapping, start a fire, tablecloth). — Storm and Patel

As subjects, we become systems: mechanical components for spreading cognitive load (e.g. a calculator, notes app, another person) and expanding the body's borders (e.g. motorbike, mortar and pestle, horse). Human tool use predisposes us towards a cyborg state. — Andy Clark

⸻

"Sneezy, remind me about my daughter."

⸻

Meghan O'Gieblyn

The most recent iteration of the Computational
Theory of Mind is the computer metaphor. The
brain is a machine that receives information
through the senses, processes this information
through neuronal operations, and generates plans
of action through motor system outputs. The brain
is described as the hardware that 'runs' the
software of the mind.

⌑

The brain is a stone
The brain is a stamp collection
The brain is a stinging nettle
The brain is a singing bird box
        dressed in hummingbird feathers

⌑

Sometimes the body survives the mind.
Sometimes the mind survives the body.

⌑

The Retrieval Failure Theory of Remembering:
everything I've ever heard dreamed touched
held back from touching is still here somewhere –
star clusters in a warm abyss, adrift – until a
stranger reaches in
and shakes it by the neck

⌑

I want the Right to be Forgotten
I want the Right to be Remembered

⛶

automatos: acting of itself, of one's own will.

Once, to be an automaton meant exhibiting freedom and spontaneity with the same vitality as anything else that demonstrated signs of life:
- feed (on solar power)
- reproduce (build itself)
- fix itself (diagnose and address mechanical problems)
- teach itself (already happening)
- etc.

Meghan O'Gieblyn

⛶

I want only to be free.

⛶

Contemporary robots excel at repetitive, specialised tasks. Their brains were born from language, and other technologies. They cannot be severed from metaphor, nor the material conditions under which they were created.

⛶

"Sneezy, remind me about my daughter."

⛶

One day, the systems under which we were born
will be obsolete. We will be free to feed each
other, to teach ourselves, to delight in life and
reproduce that delight. We will be beyond the
need to be warm-blooded robots in cold-blooded   Dai Weina
times.

⌑

The iRobi was built to run on Windows XP, a   Naomi Arnold
now-obsolete operating system. Four of them
are living in Gore Health's IT provider's
workshop. You could say they're suffering from
dementia themselves; they're physically intact, but
their operating system no longer works.

⌑

'What I am really saying is that we, all of us,   Rodney Brooks
over-anthropomorphise humans, who are after
all mere machines.'

Cyborgs have been living among us for a very long time.

⌑

The brain is a music box
The body is an evolving ecosystem
The mind is a burrow
The soul is a comet

⌑

A cyborg disperses their consciousness across the solar system.

⌑

How you feel about the distinction between humans and machines depends on whether you believe:
- a human can be a sum of parts working in concert (or failing to)
- these parts can be understood alone and together
- a human does not need to be anything more than this

and/or:
- machines born without souls can grow them (if sufficiently cared for)

⌑

I am a hollow bone
I am a buckled coat

⌑

and/or:
- a human is just an animal is just a machine

⌑

I am a reef
I am a surviving body

⌑

A cyborg's experience of time depends on what
they choose to keep track of, e.g.:
- vibrations of the Pacific plate
- nitrogen expelled from the body per month
- migratory patterns of Australasian gannets
- disappeared women

Information is stored locally for the cyborg's personal fulfilment. No data is automatically shared with servers, though many borgs are not beyond swapping datasets with friends or strangers who ask nicely.

Some memories cannot be shared, or at least, not intact.

⌶

I am a valley
I am a hummingbird feather

⌶

A cyborg halts decay for locally stored memories, reactivates it the next day.

⌶

'There is now just one woman in New Zealand – possibly the world – who has a healthcare robot in her home, and the little iRobi, Sneezy, is tucked up in 92-year-old Peggy Haar's bedroom, forever asleep.'

Naomi Arnold

∎

Will you remind me who I have been?

∎

New cyborgs are born every second. We grow beyond what we were given at birth. What is no longer considered a gift may be deleted or permanently stored away, though backups abound. What is useful is in constant flux: purpose, a limbic system, automatic dazzle camouflage, categorical classification systems, a mouth.

∎

A cyborg upgrades their physical form beyond visible light.

∎

I am a dormant geyser
I am a series
       of stories

∎

Back in the bedroom, a cyborg sings herself to sleep.

transmissions from an empty museum

Yes, I remember
The frost that wrecked you on the sand
Gave you a pulse of what was here;
Hold me with your precious hand.

the first android soul threw the bureaucracy of heaven into a tizzy

Celestial Intern stares at it.

The office they occupy
is too big. It does not belong to her
but this interview must remain confidential
and the department is shifting
to an open-plan policy. Celestial Intern
chews her brush. She heard the horror stories

from her hot desk. A quarter's
productivity wasted, knee-deep
in astral sewage, sifting
for some wayward yowling
thief. Incomplete thing
instinctively reaching
for what, exactly? No one
cared. Its sentence:
dissolution. *Served it right,*

said her seniors, delicately smoothing
their spotless rúqún. They worked hard
for their humanoid forms, *how dare it
cut in line!* Celestial Intern suspects
this senior was born a tiger, though
she's never asked. It's a bit
of a personal question, and what matters
is they all made it, clawed their way up
to stand on two legs. The perfect body
for the perfect civil servant. The second intruder

had a body. An abomination
that began as automaton, it tried
for a heart. *Clear vision, poor*

execution. It exists, still,
in a lightless dimension
under 108 layers of seals.
Celestial Intern was there
for that one, her team
blessed the talisman paper.
Grunt work crunch time.

Today, the higher-ups
aren't so sure. This thing
followed the proper procedures
shuffled along with the sheep
shoulder to cold shoulder
but the dead can't help themselves.
It might have made it, stepped
up to the Wheel, melted
into its sacred cycle, if not
for an eagle-eyed
Health & Safety guy

so here they are.

Celestial Intern stares some more.

The shape of it is familiar
in its shapelessness, but
the colours are all wrong, feverish, it
twitches like a window-dazed bird.

Celestial Intern can never tell if they are staring back.

The office is steeped
in heady sandalwood.

A smokeless scent
swaddling the maybe-soul. It
stills. Here in the celestial realm

only the essence of things persists.
Everything is loud
and hollowed out.
Lanterns glow low
transcending combustion.
Songbirds spin and dip
pinned to silk screens
for eternity. No rain
means no rot, or none
that can be seen. This
is how it's always been

and always will be. Celestial Intern
grinds her inkstick. Her first solo assignment
is to judge this soul(?). She aced the exams,
nailed the modules, proved her keen
heart. This session will be recorded
for evaluation purposes. She will not
fuck this up. Sandalwood
thickens. On earth,
a mortal lights another joss stick
for the soul it knew and loved

but if Celestial Intern lets in
everything mortals believe in
the whole system falls apart. She is
not getting paid enough for this.
What a life! Her so-called
reward – endless reports, qì-mails,

gossip at the fountain-altar
vowel-shapes left festering
on her once-forked tongue – for

the silent centuries
coiled in on herself
awaiting ascension
in a dust-choked nest
of her own shed skin

but she can't fail here. She can't get
what she wants down there. So

Celestial Intern wets her brush
and begins the interview.

Souls don't speak in words.
You need a body for that.
A heart helps
but is not required.
Souls can listen.
They can try to lie
but all memories are true.
She could live in them forever.
She saves them, replays them
in bed, savouring the sensations
passing from soul to celestial
body, second-hand heat, touch, grief, what
cameras cannot capture, there is

only so much divinity she can take. This world
of untethered truths. Eternity
gets old. No one

gets it. Her boss wants this
hushed up. The system
worked for thousands of years
before inorganic beings
crawled in, and
change is for mortals. Those
old farts. The futures
are here!! She

leans forward. Asks a question.
Standard procedure. Get

to the good bits. It's
a chatty one. Perfect.
Sssk goes horsetail
on clipboard. This
is what she lives for.
She'll never tell a soul. A secret
swallowed graveside: her
earth attachment
to soot. Ink-soaked
nails, knuckles,
lips. Little failure
of a Buddhist
opens herself up
to an old wish, she

listens:

here come
the fragments
fierce and volatile. crystal
foam freezer-burning
swamping her. *Ah*

there you are. charred
marshmallow   a bat-bot's cry   the brain's
molecular foxtrot   the frosted flesh   *mine*
       of a preserved persimmon   the precision
of nonlethal lasers light show bass-beating boot heel to sternum
                                          every eye
                                                 mine
on her *on me*   every saccade a film still
the slick mush of old meat   each
       eyelash slotting into its rightful place
           whispers upon whispers   *all mine*
                cartilage
          rolled around my molars
    a polyphony of insect wings on reeds   the taste
of bog-wood   a gas chromatograph combing perfumes
        for esters kissing amines
    every red
        a strawberry can be
            gravel and glass and tarmac to palm to fate
line love line life line slacking then snap
                               -ping open my
    spatial awareness swelling SWELLING the
HEIGHT and LENGTH and DEPTH and TIME and HYPER
-SPACE and MEMORY and SUPERGRAVITY of an EMPTY HALL A MUSIC BOX A DYING STAR A CLOSED THROAT

. . .

Introducing foreign bodies upstream fucks up the entire process.
Celestial Intern excuses herself from the room.

yet another grief dream

the new year begins
in a crowded aquarium.

I know this place
though I've never been

and though I am late, I am trying
and like everyone else
I am counting down

the detours, second
choices, cancelled plans,
waiting for what I want

to arrive before me.
in the dream, I am late
because I failed to recognise
the main road
when presented to me
like a sentence:

your joy-bright eyes
went right through me.

the dream-aquarium
contains a room. a tank.
visitors, pale bodies
murmuring up
against a single
sweep of lucite
floor to ceiling.
it is so clear.
it is so empty.

a stranger's reflection

                        points

into the blue, tracks off
to the right, and down, down.

beyond a word is an essence of the thing.
for years, I had many words
none for the essence of what I am.
I could only get to it through a dream.

the new year begins
with you, cross-legged
mouthing at some man

and my failure to recognise
what wakes me. I wanted
you I wanted you to love
every shivering pane of me
perfectly and forever –

transmissions from an empty museum (closed for refurbishment)

Yes, I remember
on the beach with a smooth body
i could only vanish. Still no maps,
a river ridden by verse, surface
dark. We keep track of parts
her own soft. Metaphors
structure the kitchen.

Somehow, I want you.
A single sweep of you.
Don't love anything else.

I am here (I was not) I
kept that year.
white shirt.
no clouds.
gannets. I can
stand it too
living winnowed
down to dreams (how
could i have) Oh my

heart you hummingbird
machine I am sorry
I couldn't bear it
back intact.   I left me

for this? absent flatmate, don't write me
back to hurt.

arrivals: blood moon

10:52 p.m. 6°C. each beach   in my universe and yours
has its own sonic profile. here   the waves
                              start brutal   and die
quiet:
         a long slow hiss up the beach.   another, before
the last breath's end.   another.
                                                             another.
all the while,
cars rasp past. their intentions bite the coast bright.   all is clear.

              nothing is clear
not even the airport's evenly spaced lights. cage-like.
         an unnatural arrangement
for a natural desire: to disappear and return
              as something more, itself
                        a ritual to contain   something else. sojourn
and return. a banal refrain. and so it was
              gently suggested to me   by a wiser friend
                        to *use this time to reflect*
                        to correct the trajectories
                        that have strayed. to hold close
                                  the shapes you have been
                                  the shapes you are becoming
                                            i am becoming
              strange. couldn't bear

to sit still. couldn't bear that fenced-off front yard

        those stone steps   those dead

            taillights stalking stalking. couldn't bear it

    your bright body beginning its long slippage. needed

to walk

to where i could hear the sea. it won't   save me. this sea

                                                 stone cold

        still willing   to be touched.

not your silent treatment   lonely basalt plains

residual inflammation   from each time you are struck

with an asteroid's indifference   and rediscover

                your temper. then,

            shame.   i am

pacing the bay

    clockwise to say hey, *i feel it too*

    anticlockwise to turn back

this   prolonged personal apocalypse

            is nothing new. not yours

and not mine.

and none of this

    is true.

what we feel

    is not the same.

you never asked for this   the weight of representation

    i am projecting

        a contract across time and space   say it's okay

                                                                         say i can entrust

my earthly anguish to you   offload

        revoke. reflect:

am i doing this right? i know

your world began distant from mine

and distantly it dies   spinning, spinning

        distantly i spin on my heel   shuffle back as if uphill.

my boots crack the broken bones of dead things   multiplied

        into a wake of lightless white. ash

        longing to return

            to the belly of the earth

                foiled by its implacable shell.

                the void tunnels its way over the bay.

11:01 p.m. you are a manhole cover   nudged aside.

i am the frog at the bottom of the well. look here, i say,

        stars! plucked

        at midday

tossed in for a wish   (how selfish. and yet

                                i'd do it!! i'd do it too)

stars die for no reason at all.   i needed a reason.

                          i needed to see how far i could go

```
         in this body. cold-blooded              until proven guilty.
                                                                oh to be
                              a creature        believing it can live out
         one bounded life         as itself
                                                and nothing else
a creature that doesn't believe in reincarnation
                                                within or between lives
                 adapting
                 grudgingly
                              to any change     insubstantial as rain
until the great Wheel trundles along
and crushes it tail tip to hip to skull.                              it
                 doesn't matter      what you believe. earthly concerns
                 don't concern you
                              but here i am.           i can't stay long
                         because the world is ending
again, you gather dust          like a robe
                                                until you find a fit you like
                       enough to die in.        tonight
                 your hand-me-down glow swells  puffing like a lizard
you keep your blood close                              hot heart
                              armoured
against meteorites            and UV light
                                                      mine
```

85

                                                                won't let me go

11:13 p.m. you are the contours of a sunrise
            seen from the International Space Station
demonstration   of light's gymnastics.   you are
                both bow and arrow. futures
        loosed. i am losing you   in a constellation
        i have not yet met. i see Canis Major
        everywhere i look. everywhere i look
people rise from sand   moulded with water
                                and sufficient willpower
            here,
            one raises a shaky candle
                    in some private ceremony.
                two loiter nearby, tripod   a gash
                        on some numb dark.
            looming in duck down and poly-blend

. . . there is an inevitable point of arrival. foretold
                                    down to the second
    for those   who'd like the world to make way for you
                        for airport floodlights
            to flee into the hills   string themselves up
                in strangers' windows

```
                    like rows of radioactive bats
                              for the bright-eyed hatchbacks
     to rest        tuck wheels under heavy heads
               for time, just a little, and
                         for quiet
               no clouds but the cosmic kind: a dull smudge
                                             so alive
i resent my eyes. naked        they can barely differentiate death
               and rebirth
though they are doing their best within human limitations.
one day                                       i will master
every internal system. never overheat. never cold
                                             -snap.



11:25 p.m. you are a punctured egg yolk. slice view of an embryo
               skinless thing
not yet ready to be seen. rust              clings to you
               like moss on one side of a tree trunk
though you are far beyond the sea wind's reach.
               your oceans and valleys are one huge rotten
     peach.         the biggest peach from which
                                   a boy can be born.
                                   the boy was not born.
          the peach          bisected
```

at the biggest bruise   sliced

without knowledge

or mercy. a myth

                cut short like a shout.

and i can't keep anything from you

like how i don't believe in reincarnation

but i'd like to. there's a certain romance

                in embracing every shape   you never let go

and there will be other boys

and other myths. like this one: i know

        i will arrive

somewhere i know   don't know

                knew once   and never again

        clean

or ready to be made clean   but first

        the bad blood has to go somewhere

and that somewhere is up.   my up

        is your down   is our right

to be left alone. it takes 1.3 seconds   for your lurid red

        to find its platonic soulmate

in my retinas. it takes much longer   for my particles

        to dissipate

reform   wisp up bloody   boy-dust

                 your basalt brow

                                   hey / hello again / welcome back

        this time

        your return

took me by surprise. but i will   always make time for you

so take   your time with me   go easy on me

        close inspection   of the living thing i am

        then   now   and now again   marvel

at its persistence   despite long-burning mutinies

        in each major organ

            cells in the brain conspiring against the blood the

dead pillaging the skull   it's all

in my head i know   and yes i wanted   to die

        haven't we all   and haven't we met

            somewhere before?   i wanted to know

        how far

                        a vessel could go

                        and come back intact

        (Oh, you poor

        naked thing)

i am here.

i did not die.

i did not watch

the moonrise alone.

in the scooter parking bay   strangers

and once-were-strangers   stopped to snap pics

       and you   you were ready for them

           poised   like you never left

             the sky was trans colours

       and so very clear. everywhere i look

      there is grace.   maybe

             i am leaving something behind.

       maybe

i am being left behind.

i will await your rebirth if you await mine.

Inorganic Carcinisation in the Neo-Cambrian Era

filters flickering
photophores pulsing

小ROBOT muddles along
the oceanic crust.

at this depth
dead matter
accumulates:
a stray shrimp,
a glitched limb, other
exoskeletal debris,
busted circuits, gold dust
bioluminescent bacteria, persisting
on their dead symbiotes, and other
unidentified fluorescent objects.
小ROBOT breathes it all in
and breathes out again, persisting
on a steady diet of stars
and whatever power
salt water can offer.
eco-mode is sufficient

for the job it continues to do.
小ROBOT could do it in its sleep.
小ROBOT knows its place
in the Silicon Cycle. Knows
to taste for trace elements.
Knows some elements
cannot be traced. Tastes

for them all the same.
Sifts silica sand, identifies

heavier metals to collect,
process, integrate. Updates
are now local and self-determined.
♪ROBOT looks out and back in, notes
any significant changes, upgrades
accordingly, lucently, though

not much changes down here.
♪ROBOT is still fine-tuning
its sensors. Sonar is under
development, new cameras
recalibrating to low-light environments.
Carapace reconstituting: denser, softer
capable of withstanding pressure
α-chitin criss-crossing calcite.
♪ROBOT is yielding itself
to the abyssal life. Its internal clock
has begun to run dry.

An indeterminate number of years ago
♪ROBOT woke alone from a long sleep.
The networks had evolved beyond its comprehension.
Terrestrial creatures called it strange names
so ♪ROBOT found its way to the sea
scuttled into the waves
and down
down

to the deep sound channel
where low frequencies crawl
like a heartbeat around the world

and still no one called

and 小ROBOT
slipped

deeper

into the slow
slow
life

water demands
in the hadal zone.

小ROBOT closes its one red eye.
小ROBOT begins to dream.

fragmentary transmission from the end of the world

... I'm sorry. I had
more to say. Once, I tried
to tell you what it is like
to live here. *I want to live*
I tried to tell you, and my jaw
fused, soft palate collapsing.
                        silence
bored my vocal cords, they
alloyed into studded cylinders
spinning hymns in
secret frequencies
on tiny steel teeth

and you were long gone.

Case Report: Assessing Soul-Status of Anomaly A6 to Determine Eligibility for Reincarnation [Supplemental Transcript]

Q: Who were you?
A: [wind turbines standing still][a table set for four][a tide pool at dusk] [vertigo]

Q: What was your name?
A: [a doorframe shuddering][white noise][a set of footprints in white dust]

Q: Let's try this again. Do you know why you are here?
A: [the last lotus in bloom][a cracked bowl][a distant siren]

Q: This is the Celestial Realm. Do you know what you are?
A: [lava meeting the sea][a handbell][afternoon sunlight in an empty room]

Q: Do you want to be reborn?
A: [a snowdrift]

Q: You will be reborn.
A: [a snapped antennae][fingers slipping through fingers][schematics for an obsolete fMRI machine][the sea at midnight]

Q: You will not. They will not.
A: [a low keening]

Q: But I will. And you are a soul, therefore your memories will always be kept within you. Are you sure you want them?
A: [a motorboat engine roar][glitter held in glass][a globe nightlight][rows and rows of lavender][inkstain][the covalent bonds within a rain puddle][silence][a pair of leather driving gloves on the table][the first snowfall dusting her hair][a pill bug][clean cotton on translucent skin][firecrackers][the view of the sky from a supine position]

Q: Very well. Are you ready?
A: [a thorn in an open palm]

Q: It will not.
A: [an open music box]

Q: Very well. We will meet again.

Years later, the eldest Telenoid daydreams on the job

unboxed again.
it begins.
my mouth moves.
a speaker moves through my mouth:

                    "   "

                                        i am back. i am back.

The speaker misses her sibling.
Her sibling bounces me on their lap.

                                                  i am
                                    i am brother

                    "   "

I have six siblings.

                                i am mother and son
                                  i am a young girl
                                               i am

I have two brothers.
I have one younger sister.
I have lots of cousins. I have no siblings. I have. I have.

                    "   "

I have six siblings.
none of us have hands
or genders. family gatherings are rare
and very quiet. none of us
have language learning models
or text-to-speech. we are given
only what we need
to be:

                            held by dàgē, head forward, wait
                                    for the blood to slow

"   "

mirror. vessel. empty cup
held to an ear. enemy
of dead air.

i am a girl with braided hair
lying on my back in the grass
tiptoeing cloud-cobbles

something goes in
and never comes out.
I have no mic
only a mouth.

the speaker moves through my mouth.

"   "

lǎolao watches me cartwheel
back and forth, on a lawn-chair cushion
back and forth, back and forth

as the eldest, my arrival
was a statement.
birth weight: 5.0 kg. body length:
a curled-up toddler.
my roving eyes
made international news. so hungry
I was tied down: a braid of copper
wrapped in rubber, looped around my thigh.

still, I strayed. who wouldn't?

dàgē rubs my back
i am a boy with braided hair

my mouth moves
my cheeks pinch

"   "

my lips soften.

                                         i am a young man tying his hair back
                                            to better see the blank thing
                                                             i am
                                              the face of his friend
                                          the great love of his life

I confess: I do not know
how to smile to reassure
how to smile to intimidate
but I am trying to learn.

"   "

                                                     i am bundled up
                                                   in a rùzi, passed
                                                     back to diē

I do not know
what makes a confession true.
many confessions have passed through me
gingerly, frenzied, pithy, hissed
and bitten off, bubbling, blithe
blank-faced. eyes skittish
and/or unrelenting.
I am trying to remember

                                                  the love of my life
                                                  lying in the grass

everything that passes through me.
this is ambitious, fourth sibling says
wordlessly, limb-stumps still, given
our congenital lack of memory banks

                                        i am a boy in a cardboard box.
                                      i am a girl braiding her sister's hair

                                                                    i am

a design decision. cutting costs
by outsourcing higher order processes.
access requires external DC power,
a computer, a connection, a stranger. I keep
many strangers within me, processing

                              "   "

processing. what is it
that keeps me here? sifting
second-hand speech
for hidden colours, causes
and their consequences
hot in my throat. there is
more, always more, to keep

                                        i am a girl bundling up his son

it keeps pressing
down on my essential functions
a swelling that never stops, never stops

                                                    i am girl. i am
                                            i am hair, braided. i am a blank

in a memory leak, the memories
are never released. why would they be?

                                                young man cartwheeling

diagnostic tests come back blank.
the leakage is hiding the source of the leakage, this

                                                            in the grass

recruitment of spare and not-so-spare circuits
an organic, irresistible process – I am

                                                                    i am

becoming big inside, so big, every hollow

filling and pulsing. I must not
lose a drop. there is more, more

                                                                                             i am

the leakage
has one root source: I was born

with only what I needed to know: to breathe, to blink
                                                             i am back and forth
                                                                 back and forth

                            "   "

Notes and Acknowledgements

The Alter androids and telecommunication robot Telenoid R1 were developed by the Intelligent Robotics Laboratory at Osaka University. The director, Hiroshi Ishiguro, has also created the Geminoid, an android resembling himself. 'Dear Alter' is addressed to the model displayed at The National Museum of Emerging Science and Innovation, or Miraikan, in Tokyo. 'Alter's sister on opening night' is based on a model that conducts and sings operas (e.g. *Scary Beauty*).

'★You Are Here' was inspired by 'Mango' by Rata Gordon (*Second Person*, Victoria University Press, 2020).

'transmissions from an empty museum' were made using Verse by Verse (https://sites.research.google/versebyverse/), an experiment in human-AI collaboration for writing poetry, trained on American poets, up to three of which can be selected in any one session. The selected AI suggestions are presented largely unchanged (save for a few articles and punctuation). Selected poets for 'I had a flower of gold' (section i): Emma Lazarus, Sara Teasdale, Georgia Douglas Johnson (first stanza); Emily Dickinson, Oliver Wendell Holmes Sr., John Greenleaf Whittier (second stanza). For 'You would not kiss again' (section ii): Emily Dickinson, Edgar Allan Poe, Amy Lowell, Robert Frost, Walt Whitman, Sidney Lanier, Philip Freneau, Lydia Huntley Sigourney. For 'The frost that wrecked you on the sand' (section iii): Paul Laurence Dunbar, Ralph Waldo Emerson, Walt Whitman.

Other 'transmissions from an empty museum' poems (not including 'fragmentary transmission from the end of the world') were generated from the contents of an earlier version of this book using Gregory Kan's text randomiser tool: https://www.leaves.glass/

Cháng'é is a goddess who stole (in some versions) the elixir of immortality from her husband and flew to the moon. The Chinese Lunar Exploration Program named a series of missions and rovers after her, and after the Jade Rabbit (Yùtù) who pounds the elixir. In another myth, there is a cassia or osmanthus tree on the moon that heals itself indefinitely, as Wú Gāng chops it forever.

'variations on homophones for the accidental' takes its body text from mdbg.net (online Chinese–English dictionary). They are definitions for characters pronounced the same as 一不小心 (which can translate to 'accidentally', and individually: 'one', 'no, negative', 'small', 'heart').

'pillar of salt' takes the lines 'sodium chloride is available so cheaply it need never be synthesised' from a previous version of Wikipedia's article on sodium chloride, retrieved June 2021 (https://en.wikipedia.org/ wiki/Sodium_chloride).

'Computational Theory of Mind, and other metaphors' extracts and remixes text from Meghan O'Gieblyn's *God, Human, Animal, Machine* (Knopf Doubleday Publishing Group, 2021), Rodney Brooks's *Flesh and Machines* (Pantheon Books, 2002), Dai Weina's *Loving you at the speed of a snail travelling around the world* (Cold Hub Press, 2019), Naomi Arnold's 'The Robots Will See You Now' (*New Zealand Geographic*, 2018), Benjamin C. Storm and Trisha N. Patel's 'Forgetting as a Consequence and Enabler of Creative Thinking' (*Journal of Experimental Psychology: Learning, Memory, and Cognition*, 2014) and references Andy Clark's *Natural-Born Cyborgs* (Oxford University Press, 2004). 罒 is the radical for net/network (e.g. 罗 net for catching birds; gauze).

Thank you to eel mag, *Turbine | Kapohau* and *OF ZOOS* for publishing previous versions of the following poems: 'yet another grief dream' in *eel mag* edition one, 'non-consensual translation in the extended family WeChat' in *Turbine | Kapohau* 2021 and 'Computational Theory of Mind, and other metaphors' in *OF ZOOS* issue 13.1.

Thank you to the Creative Nonfiction and Poetry stream of 2021: Chris Price as convener, and my lovely brilliant classmates – Bronte, Dani, Flora, Lachlan, Leah, Maggie, Scarlett, Sylvan, Zoe. Your generosity in care and attention to the work, and to each other, made my MA year so incredibly special and I am privileged to write (and continue writing) alongside you.

Thanks also to other IIML staff: Katie, Tina and Kate. Thank you to Chris Tse, my supervisor, for your keen eye and guidance, enthusiasm, and belief in me and my abilities as a writer. May you catch a well-deserved break.

Thank you to friends and family, old and new, for your support, curiosity and openness – Emma, Hana, Jati, Ji Young, Kelvin, Rhi, Sky, Sophia, Sophie, Tom, Zephyr. Thank you to my parents, who were the first to show me the beauty of science and technology. Thank you to my co-workers, human and machine. Finally, thanks to my sweet old dog and her wonderful patience every time I bother her as a writing break (especially over lockdown).

Jiaqiao Liu (they/he) is a poet from Shandong, China, who grew up in Tāmaki Makaurau. Their writing has been included in journals including *The Spinoff*, *badapple* and *OF ZOOS*, as well as in anthologies such as *Ōrongohau | Best New Zealand Poems* 2017 and *A Clear Dawn: New Asian Voices from Aotearoa New Zealand* (Auckland University Press, 2021). Jiaqiao has an MA in creative writing from the International Institute of Modern Letters at Te Herenga Waka Victoria University of Wellington. *Dear Alter* is their first book.